A Dorling Kindersley Book

Text Terry Martin
Project Editor Mary Atkinson
Senior Art Editor Jane Horne
Deputy Managing Editor Mary Ling
Production Louise Barratt
Consultant Theresa Greenaway
Picture Researcher Lorna Ainger

Additional photography by Peter Anderson, Jane Burton, Peter Chadwick,
Geoff Dann, Mike Dunning, Steve Gorton, Frank Greenaway, Dave King,
Tracy Morgan, Stephen Oliver, Stephen Shott, Kim Taylor, Matthew Ward,
Jerry Young

First published in Great Britain in 1996
by Dorling Kindersley Limited,
9 Henrietta Street, London WC2E 8PS

Colour reproduction by Chromagraphics, Singapore
Printed and bound in Italy by L.E.G.O.

The publisher would like to thank the following for
their kind permission to reproduce their photographs:
Bruce Coleman: Jane Burton 8-9c, 14-15c, Adrian Davies 20-21br, Francisco J.
Erize 12-13c, Jeff Foott Productions 12bl, Hwange N. P. back cover c, 6-7c,
Harald Lange 20-21c, Hans Reinhard front cover c, 16-17c, 18-19c, Kim Taylor
10-11c; The Image Bank: John W. Banagan Endpapers

Contents

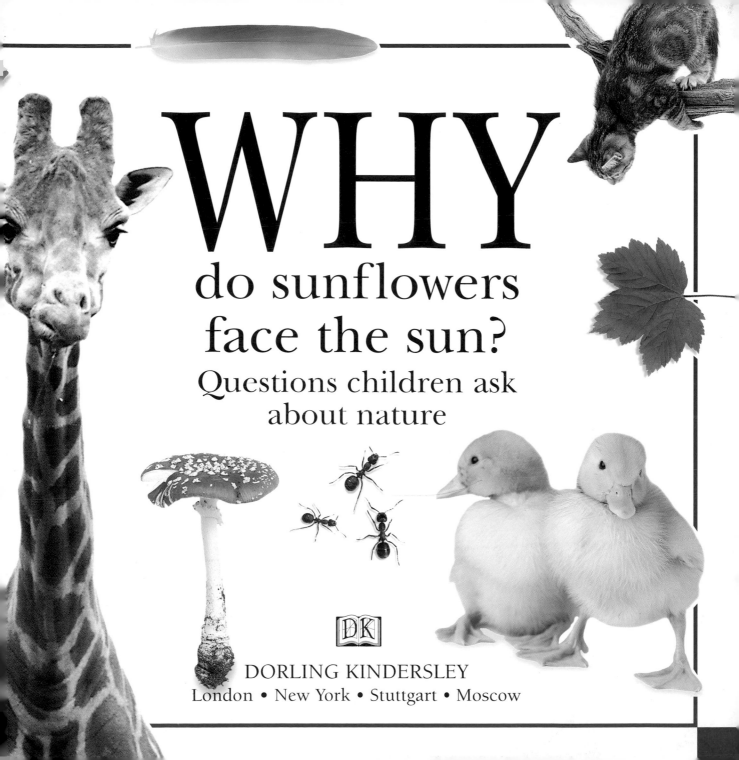

WHY

do sunflowers face the sun?

Questions children ask about nature

DK

DORLING KINDERSLEY

London • New York • Stuttgart • Moscow

Why do elephants

An elephant's long nose does more than smell. It acts as a trumpet, a hose, a snorkel, a hand to pluck leaves, and an arm to reach up high or to lift heavy objects.

Why don't polar bears get cold?
In the harsh, icy Arctic, polar bears can hunt for hours in freezing cold water. The bulky layers of fat under their thick, oily fur coats keep them warm.

have long trunks?

Why do giraffes have long necks?
The world's longest neck doesn't just give a giraffe a great view, it also allows it to munch tasty leaves high on the tops of tall trees.

Why don't cats hurt

Cats are very fast and supple. If they fall, they quickly twist around to land on their feet. They also have special leg joints that absorb the shock of hitting the hard ground.

Why are rabbits' ears so big?
Rabbits are expert ear wigglers. Their big, sensitive ears can

themselves when they fall?

Why do dogs pant?
A dog pants and flops out its long, sloppy tongue to cool down. Water drying off its tongue cools a dog in the same way that sweat cools us.

move together or one at a time, to pick up the slightest sound of danger.

Feathers make good flying jackets. They're not only warm, they're also lightweight, and have curved shapes that catch the wind, helping birds to fly.

Why do cockerels crow at dawn?
The cockerel gives an ear-splitting dawn performance to remind everyone that he's number one – the strongest male in the roost.

have feathers?

Why do ducks have webbed feet?
Ducks have amazing "paddle power". Their webbed feet propel them speedily through water like the oars on a boat.

Why do crabs walk

To avoid a messy tangle of eight, long legs, crabs scuttle sideways — especially during fast getaways. Their front legs pull, and their back legs push. Then, zoom, they're off.

Why do whales spurt water?
Whales take huge lungfuls of ai
before diving underwater. Unlik
fish, they must come back up to

sideways?

Why don't fish drown?
Like us, fish need to breathe oxygen. But while our lungs are designed to take oxygen out of the air, fishes' gills are able to take oxygen out of water.

take another breath. When they exhale, warm, moist air snorts out of their nostril, or blowhole, turning into a fountain of water and air.

Why do snails carry

A snail's shell is like a caravan – a mobile home that it carries around. Whenever it senses danger, it quickly curls up inside its shell.

Why don't flies fall when they walk upside-down?
A fly's sharp claws are no use on a smooth upside-down surface like a ceiling. But it also has a hairy pad on each foot that can grip like a plumber's suction cup.

shells on their backs?

Why do ants travel in lines?
After discovering food, an ant rushes back to
ts nest, leaving a smelly trail behind it. Other
ants then follow their noses to find the food.

Why don't worms have legs?
Earthworms live underground,
creating deep tunnels as they
wriggle about. Their long, thin,
legless bodies have
stiff bristles and
strong muscles
that are
perfect
for
pushing
through soil.

15

Why do trees

Like tiny solar panels, leaves soak up sunlight energy to make the food a tree needs to grow.

Why do pine trees have cones?
Pine trees take a long time to grow their soft, delicate seeds. The seeds grow inside cones, where they're protected from rain and hungry animals by the cone's woody scales.

have leaves?

Why does a tree stump have lots of rings?
Each year's spring growth spurt produces another ring inside a tree trunk. By counting these rings, you can work out a tree's age.

Why do sunflowers turn

Sunflowers' beautiful, yellow heads and green leaves follow the sun across the sky, making warm landing pads for bees and catching lots of energy-giving light.

Why do plants have to be watered?
Next time it rains, think about the plants outside. They use rainwater to

towards the sun?

Why do cactuses have prickles?
Cactuses are the roughest, toughest plants in the desert. Their sharp prickles protect them from hungry animals and collect precious water from dewdrops.

...ake food and to hold up their ...aves. Indoor plants would die if we ...idn't give their thirsty roots a drink.

Why can't I eat

Toadstools might look like mushrooms, but many are highly poisonous. These red and white toadstools are some of the deadliest of all.

Why do fungi grow on tree stumps?
Many fungi feed on rotting trees. As they eat, they grow deep into the wood, helping to break it down.

toadstools?

Why do some fungi have frilly gills?
Gills are launching pads for millions of tiny seed-like spores, which may soon grow into new fungi.

Why does food go mouldy?
A mould is a type of fungus. Its tiny spores float in the air like specks of dust. When a spore lands on food, it grows into another mould.